GET WELL SOON

Stomach Bug

Anita Ganeri and

Beatriz Castro

Enslow PUBLISHING

Published in 2025 by Enslow Publishing, LLC
2544 Clinton Street
Buffalo, NY 14224

First published in Great Britain in 2023 by Hodder & Stoughton

Series editor: Julia Bird
Illustrator: Beatriz Castro
Design: Collaborate

Manufactured in the United States of America

CPSIA compliance information: Batch #CSENS25: For further information contact Enslow Publishing LLC, New York, New York at 1-800-398-2504.

Please visit our website, www.enslowpublishing.com. For a free color catalog of all our high-quality books, call toll free 1-800-398-2504 or fax 1-877-980-4454.

Cataloging-in-Publication Data

Names: Ganeri, Anita, 1961-. | Castro, Beatriz.
Title: Stomach bug / by Anita Ganeri and Beatriz Castro.
Description: Buffalo, NY : Enslow Publishing, 2025. | Series: Get well soon
Identifiers: ISBN 9781978538719 (pbk.) |
ISBN 9781978538726 (library bound) | ISBN 9781978538733 (ebook)
Subjects: LCSH: Gastroenteritis--Juvenile literature--Miscellanea. | Digestion--Juvenile literature. | Digestive organs--Juvenile literature. | Vomiting--Juvenile literature.
Classification: LCC RC840.G3 G24 2025 | DDC 616.3'3--dc23

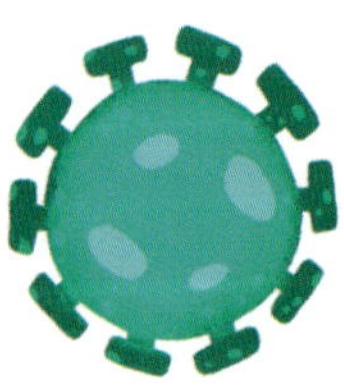

Find us on

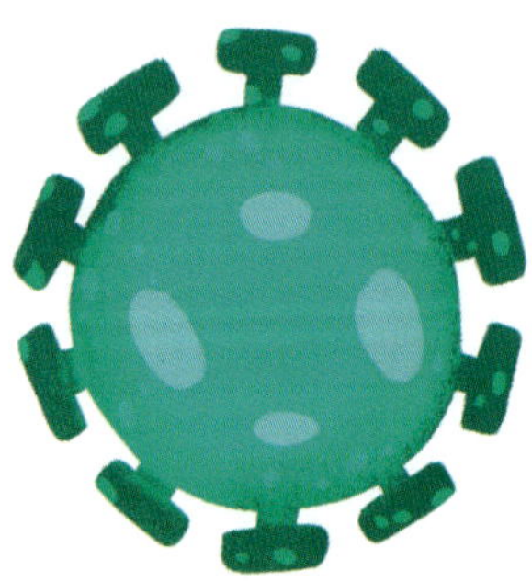

GET WELL SOON

Stomach Bug

Hello there. My name's Tom, and this book is all about the time I got a stomach bug. It was horrible. I felt really sick, but luckily, it didn't last for too long.

My mom soon helped me to feel better. And I got a few days off school!

This book has information and advice about having a stomach bug to help you and your parents or caregivers. On the following pages, you can find out:

What is a stomach bug?

Why do you feel sick?

What can make you better?

Can you give it to other people?

This book is about having a stomach bug, an illness called gastroenteritis. It means having a stomachache, throwing up, and sometimes having diarrhea (runny poop).

Tom's mom knocks on his bedroom door.

Tom opens his eyes. He slowly sits up in bed. His head aches and his legs feel a bit wobbly. He also feels a bit sick.

Tom gets dressed and goes downstairs for breakfast. He only manages to eat a few bites of toast. His mom looks worried.

After breakfast, Tom sets off for school. Halfway down the street, he hears his mom calling after him.

Tom goes back to grab his lunch box. He doesn't think he'll be able to eat his packed lunch today. Even thinking about food makes him feel ill.

As the morning goes on, Tom feels more and more sick. His headache is getting worse, and he starts feeling hot, and then cold. Science is usually his favorite class, but he's struggling to concentrate today.

At lunchtime, Tom heads for the dining hall. His mom has made cheese and tomato sandwiches. They're usually his favorite. But today, he only manages to force down a few bites.

Afterwards, Tom and his friend, Roshan, go to the big bake sale. The tables are piled high with delicious cakes and cookies. All the money raised is going to charity.

Tom takes a bite of his cake. But he soon realizes he's made a BIG mistake! His tummy starts making strange, gurgling noises. He dashes off the bathroom to be sick.

Roshan rushes off to tell his teacher, Miss Lindsay, about poor Tom. He wonders if he's going to be sick, too, but he feels fine after eating his cake.

Tom's mom comes to pick him up. He's feeling really ill now. His tummy's gurgling, and he keeps having to run to the bathroom with diarrhea.

Back home, Tom goes to bed. His mom puts an old bowl by his bed in case he needs to be sick again.

Then Mom goes downstairs to read up on the health advice on gastroenteritis.

Gastroenteritis

What is it?

- It's a very common kind of stomach upset
- It's caused by bugs, called viruses or bacteria
- These can affect your tummy so it doesn't work properly.

What are the symptoms?

- Feeling or being sick
- Diarrhea
- You may also need to poop more often than usual
- Stomachache
- Gurgling noises from your tummy.

You may also:

- Feel hot, then cold
- Have a headache
- Have aching muscles
- Not feel hungry.

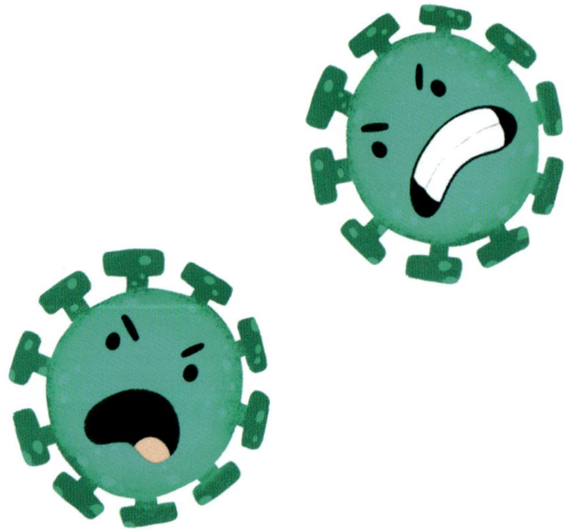

Mom looks up how to care for someone who has gastroenteritis. Luckily, it usually clears up on its own, and Tom should feel much better in a few days.

But there are some things that can help a person to recover from a stomach bug:

- Give them plenty of water to drink to keep them from getting dehydrated (see next page).

- Make sure they get plenty of rest.

- If they feel hungry, give them small amounts of plain foods, such as rice, soup, pasta, or bread.

- If they're feeling hot and achy, give them acetaminophen (there's liquid acetaminophen for children). Read the instructions carefully and make sure they only take the recommended dose.

Mom gets a glass of water and takes it upstairs for Tom.

Dehydration - did you know?

- When you throw up or have diarrhea, your body loses lots of water.

- If you don't replace the water you lose, it can make you very ill.

- You might feel dizzy, have a dry mouth, or pee less than usual.

- You should drink plenty of fluids - plain water is best.

- Don't drink fizzy drinks or fruit juice - it can make diarrhea worse.

By the evening, Tom is feeling a bit better.
His tummy doesn't hurt so much, and he
hasn't thrown up again.

By the next day, Tom is almost back to normal.

The bugs that cause gastroenteritis can spread very easily from person to person. Tom needs to stay home from school for another two days to make sure his classmates don't catch the illness from him.

Luckily, Mom has bought him a new video game ...

DID YOU KNOW?

When you have gastroenteritis, you can easily spread the illness to other people.

Someone could catch your stomach bug by:

• Shaking or holding your hand, if you've got the bug on your hands.

• Being too close to you, if you have tiny germs in your breath.

• Touching an object or a surface that you've touched.

• Sharing towels or utensils.

• Eating food that you've touched.

If you have a stomach bug, you are most likely to spread it from when you start feeling ill to at least two days after all your symptoms are gone. You should stay home from school, so that there's less risk of passing it on.

A few days later, Tom is feeling MUCH better. He hasn't thrown up or had diarrhea for three days.

Tom gets dressed and comes down for breakfast.

Tom washes his hands and has some toast.
Then he eats a bowl of cereal.

After breakfast, Tom sets off for school. Halfway down the street, he hears his mom calling after him.

Tom goes back to grab his lunch box. This time, he's looking forward to his cheese and tomato sandwich.

In the school playground, he bumps into Roshan.

QUIZ

Now that you've reached the end of the book, how much do you think you know about stomach bugs? Try this quick quiz to find out.

1. What's another name for a stomach bug?
a) Tonsillitis
b) Chicken pox
c) Gastroenteritis

2. Which of these are signs of a stomach bug?
a) Feeling sick
b) Feeling hot
c) Having diarrhea

3. What causes a stomach bug?
a) Eating too much
b) Viruses
c) Bacteria

4. Which of these will help you feel better?
a) Drinking water
b) Drinking juice
c) Drinking milk

5. How can you pass a stomach bug on?
a) Touching someone's hand
b) Sharing towels or utensils
c) Getting too close

Answers:
1.c); 2. All of them; 3. b) & c); 4. a); 5. All of them

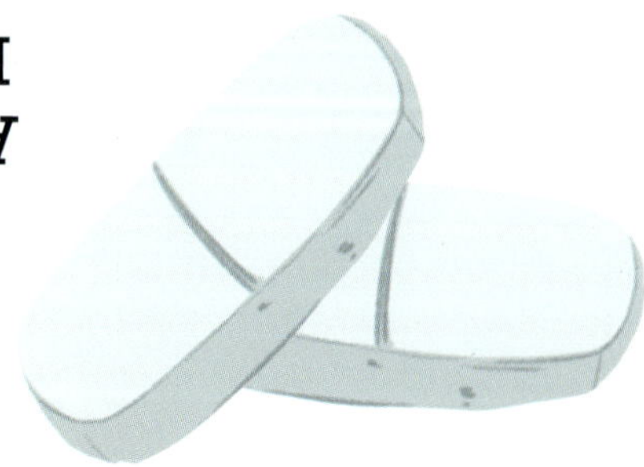

USEFUL WORDS

bacteria
Types of bugs (germs) that can get inside your body and make you ill.

charity
A group that helps people or animals in need.

concentrate
To give your full attention to something.

dehydrated
Not having enough water in your body so you feel ill or weak.

diarrhea
Poop that is softer and more liquid than usual.

gastroenteritis
Another name for a stomach bug.

particles
Tiny pieces of something.

symptoms
The signs that you have an illness.

viruses
Types of bugs (germs) that can get inside your body and make you ill.

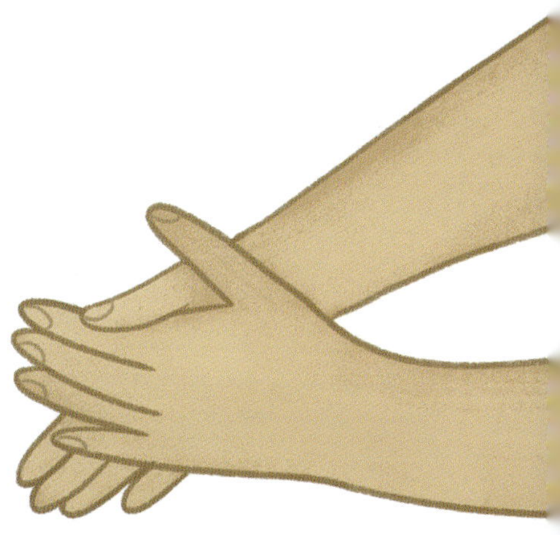

ADVICE FOR PARENTS AND CAREGIVERS

Children usually recover from gastroenteritis on their own. Their symptoms should improve after a few days, and you don't normally need to get medical advice. Don't take the child into a doctor's office or pharmacy in case they are still infectious.

Call your doctor for advice if:

- The child has been vomiting for more than two days or has had diarrhea for more than seven days.

- They feel drowsy, dizzy, or aren't peeing much – they might be dehydrated.

- There is any blood in their diarrhea.

- If they have green or yellow-green vomit.

- They can't keep any food or fluids down, and keep being sick.

- They have a temperature of over 100°F (38°C).

- They have any other medical conditions that make infections more likely.

MORE INFORMATION

https://kidshealth.org/en/parents/gastroenteritis.html
Lots of information for your parents or caregivers about what to do if you have a stomach bug.

BOOKS

Life's Little Bugs: Tummy Bug by T. Stubbs (2016)
Why Do I Vomit? by Emilie Dufresne (Secret Books, 2020)

INDEX

acetaminophen 17

bacteria 16

being sick 5, 11, 14, 20, 24

bugs 16, 21, 23

dehydration 17, 18–19, 30

diarrhea 13, 16, 24, 30

feeling sick 6, 8

headache 6, 9, 16

stomachache 5, 16, 20

stomach bug (gastroenteritis) 4, 5, 12, 15, 16–17, 21, 22, 23

- **catching** 22–23
- **complications** 30
- **spreading** 22–23
- **symptoms** 16, 23
- **treating** 17

viruses 16

washing hands 25